Aiming for Progress in
Reading

Book 1
Second Edition

William Collins' dream of knowledge for all began with the publication of his first book in 1819. A self-educated mill worker, he not only enriched millions of lives, but also founded a flourishing publishing house. Today, staying true to this spirit, Collins books are packed with inspiration, innovation and practical expertise. They place you at the centre of a world of possibility and give you exactly what you need to explore it.

Collins. Freedom to teach.

Published by Collins
An imprint of HarperCollins*Publishers*
77–85 Fulham Palace Road
Hammersmith
London
W6 8JB

Browse the complete Collins catalogue at
www.collins.co.uk

10 9 8 7 6 5 4 3 2 1
ISBN 978-0-00-754749-4

British Library Cataloguing in Publication Data
A Catalogue record for this publication is available from the British Library.

Commissioned by Catherine Martin
Project managed by Rachel Minay
Edited in-house by Alicia Higgins
Proofread by Kelly Davis
Designed by Joerg Hartmannsgruber
Typeset by G Brasnett, Cambridge
Cover design by Angela English
Production by Rebecca Evans
Printed and bound by L.E.G.O S.p.A. Italy

With thanks to Jackie Newman.

Packaged for HarperCollins by
White-Thomson Publishing Ltd.
www.wtpub.co.uk
+44 (0) 843 208 7460

Acknowledgements
The publishers gratefully acknowledge the permissions granted to reproduce copyright material in this book. While every effort has been made to trace and contact copyright holders, where this has not been possible the publishers will be pleased to make the necessary arrangements at the first opportunity.

'Dad You're Not Funny' poem taken from Dad You're Not Funny by Steve Turner, published by Lion Hudson plc, 1999. ©1999 Steve Turner. Used with permission of Lion Hudson plc (pp 6–7); extract from *The Great Trek* reproduced with the permission of Nelson Thornes Ltd from New Spirals: The Great Trek, James Rigg, ISBN 0-7487-90005-5 first published in 2004 (p 16); extracts from *Point Danger* by Catherine MacPhail. Reprinted by permission of HarperCollins Publishers Ltd ©2012 Catherine MacPhail (pp 22, 24); 'Salford Road' by Gareth Owen, from *Salford Road and other poems*. © Gareth Owen. Reprinted with permission of Rogers Coleridge & White Ltd (pp 28, 29, 30); 'Conversation Piece' by Gareth Owen, from *Salford Road and other poems*. © Gareth Owen. Reprinted with permission of Rogers Coleridge & White Ltd (pp 32–33); extract from *The Mighty Skink* by Paul Shipton, reproduced by permission of Oxford University Press (pp 42–44); 'In Ancient Time' by Michael Morpurgo, from Centuries of Stories, reprinted by permission of HarperCollins Publishers Ltd © 2009 Michael Morpurgo (p 73).

The publishers would like to thank the following for permission to reproduce pictures in these pages:

Cover image and p 1 Svetlana Lukienko/Shutterstock

(t = top, b = bottom, r = right, l = left)

p 5 dinosmichail/Shutterstock, p 6 Kzenon/Shutterstock, p 7 Kzenon/Shutterstock, p 8 Luciano Mortula/Shutterstock, p 9 Kzenon/Shutterstock, p 10 Glen Perotte/Getty Images, p 11 Glen Perotte/Getty Images, p 12 S.Borisov/Shutterstock, p 13t Dudarev Mikhail/Shutterstock, p 13b PathDoc/Shutterstock, p 15 Sebastien Burel/Shutterstock, p 16 Stanislav Fosenbauer/Shutterstock, p 17 Neftali/Shutterstock, p 18 javarman/Shutterstock, p 19 Sebastien Burel/Shutterstock, p 20tl Sabphoto/Shutterstock, p 20tr Stuart Monk/Shutterstock, p 20bl CandyBox Images/Shutterstock, p 20br Jason Stitt/Shutterstock, p 21 otsphoto/Shutterstock, pp 22-25 Illustrations from *Point Danger* © HarperCollins Publications Limited 2012 Iva Sasheva and Catherine MacPhail, p 27 Poznukhov Yuriy/Shutterstock, p 28 Tom Gowanlock/Shutterstock, p 29 Petrenko Andriy/Shutterstock, p 30 Poznukhov Yuriy/Shutterstock, p 32 michaeljung/Shutterstock, p 33 rui vale sousa/Shutterstock, p 34 Nancy Hixson/Shutterstock, p 35 michaeljung/Shutterstock, p 36 Nadezhda V. Kulagina/Shutterstock, p 37 Chester Tugwell/Shutterstock, p 38 Nadezhda V. Kulagina/Shutterstock, p 39 Nadezhda V. Kulagina/Shutterstock, p 41 stevenku/Shutterstock, p 42 Vitalez/Shutterstock, p 44 Dmitry Laudin/Shutterstock, p 45 tratong/Shutterstock, p 46 lithian/Shutterstock, p 47 lithian/Shutterstock, p 48 Tyler Olson/Shutterstock, p 49 lithian/Shutterstock, p 50 1000 Words/Shutterstock, p 51 lithian/Shutterstock, p 53 Elena Schweitzer/Shutterstock, p 54 xpixel/Shutterstock, p 55 Blue Lantern Studio/Corbis, p 56 xpixel/Shutterstock, p 57 Blue Lantern Studio/Corbis, p 58t Elena Schweitzer/Shutterstock, p 58b Elena Schweitzer/Shutterstock, p 59 Ivan Ponomarev/Shutterstock, p 60 imging/Shutterstock, p 61l Maridav/Shutterstock, p 61r Hintau Aliaksei/Shutterstock, p 62 Andresr/Shutterstock, p 63 Alexey Rozhanovsky/Shutterstock, p 65 Syda Productions/Shutterstock, p 66 epa european pressphoto agency b.v./Alamy, p 67 Art_man/Shutterstock, p 68 Dario Lo Presti/Shutterstock, p 69 Syda Productions/Shutterstock, p 71 Angela Harburn/Shutterstock, p 72tl Reprinted by permission of HarperCollins Publishers Ltd © 2012 Dan Tunstall, p 72tr and p 72br Reprinted by permission of HarperCollins Publishers Ltd © 2012 Alan Gibbons and Robbie Gibbons, p72bl Reprinted by permission of HarperCollins Publishers Ltd © 2012 Gareth Calway, p 73 Photo Image/Shutterstock, p 74t Roman Sulla/Shutterstock, p 74b Sergei Butorin/Shutterstock, p 75 Angela Harburn/Shutterstock, p 76 Chris Herring/Loop Images/SuperStock, p 77 Peter Dedeurwaerder/Shutterstock.

Contents

1

Chapter 1

Use a range of strategies, including accurate decoding of text, to read for meaning

What's it all about?

Reading with understanding and confidence.

In this chapter you will learn how to

- use a range of strategies to read tricky words

- read independently and with understanding

- read with confidence and expression.

Use a range of strategies to read tricky words

Your teacher will read this poem to you:

Dad, you're not funny!

A few of my mates
Come around to our place,
And you're at the door
With that grin on your face.
You know that I know
You're a really good bloke,
But I'll curl up and die
If you tell us a joke!

We don't want to hear
About your days at school,
We don't want to watch
You try to be cool.
We don't want to know
How the world used to be.
We don't want to see
Those videos of me!

We don't want to laugh
At your riddles and rhymes,
At musty old tales
We've heard fifty times.
We don't want a quiz
Where we have to compete,
We don't want to guess
Why the hen crossed the street.

Please don't perform
That ridiculous dance
Like you did on the night
We went out to France.
Don't do impressions
Of pop stars on drugs.
Whatever you do
Don't swamp me with hugs!

So Dad, don't come in,
Your jokes are so dated
I often pretend
That we're not related.
I'd pay you to hide
If I had my own money,
The simple truth is –
Dad, you're not funny!

by Steve Turner

1 **What do you think the poem is about?**

How does it work?

You can use strategies to help work out what is happening in the poem:

- Look at the pictures. Do they give you any clues?

- Are there some words you know well in the poem? Can you understand what is going on from those words?

- Can you sound out the words you do not know?

- Are there words within longer words that you know?

Now you try it

Re-read the poem to yourself.

2 What did the son find embarrassing about the night they went out to France?

3 What does the son say he would do if he had his own money?

4 Do you think it is a funny poem? If so, what lines make the poem funny?

Use a range of strategies, including accurate decoding of text, to read for meaning

5 Work with a partner. Write bullet points about what happens in the poem, using your own words. For example, in the first verse you might jot down the following:

- Dad is at the door grinning at the son's friends.

- The son is worried he's about to tell a corny joke.

Check your progress

Good progress ⟫

I can use some strategies to help me read difficult words.

Excellent progress ⟫⟫

I can use a range of strategies to help me read with confidence.

Read independently and with understanding

Listen to your teacher read the story and spot words you do not know:

The Hood Gang

They all wore the same jackets. Their jackets were black. I could not see their faces. I did not know any of them. They all wore their hoods up. They were the Hood Gang. People talked about them at school. They were tough. They did things at night. They broke into shops. They stole money. I knew they would get caught. Yes, one day they would get caught.

1 Discuss with your partner how you could read any words you are not sure of.

2 Jot down what you know about the Hood Gang.

3 Read *The Hood Gang* again, this time to yourself. Copy and complete the following three sentences to answer the questions.

a) What colour jackets did the gang wear?

> The jackets were…

b) What was the gang called?

> The gang was called the…

c) What does the writer think will happen to them?

> The writer thinks the gang will…

Apply your skills

4 Look at the story again. Copy out the sentences that you know are true.

a) The gang leader was called Jake.

b) People talked about the gang at school.

c) The gang stole money.

d) The gang lived in Leeds.

e) The gang was tough.

f) The gang carried guns.

Check your progress

Good progress 》

I can listen to a story and work out what some difficult words mean.

Excellent progress 》

I can read independently and work out how to say unfamiliar words.

Read with confidence and expression

1 Read the story below aloud to a partner:

- Make sure your partner can hear you.
- Remember to pause at each full stop.
- Read the story so that it flows and it is interesting for your partner to hear.

City Kids

We're city kids. We like bright lights and we're used to noise.

We know the sounds of the city. We're used to beeping horns from passing cars. We know all about sellers flogging their newspapers. We know all about the busy markets – 'Five apples for a pound. Come on, Missus.'

Each night we see the bright lights from the theatres and the bright shops selling everything from watches to bargain toys.

Mr Martell took us into the country for a two-day school trip.

When we arrived, it was pitch black and I couldn't see my hand in front of my face.

He handed us a torch each and told us we were going on a night hike.

If you think it's quiet in the country, think again! We heard rustling in the hedges and a cow mooed in the field beside us.

I admit I was a bit scared. I made sure I kept close to Mr Martell... We all did... just in case! You never know what's out there!

How does it work?

As you become more confident in your reading, you can also change the expression (feeling) in your voice to make the story seem more exciting. For example, you could use a different voice for the market seller and express how the narrator feels in each part of the story.

You never know what's out there!

Now you try it

2 With a different partner, read the story again. Use lots of expression in your voice to show how the narrator feels.

Apply your skills

3 Finally, read the story to your first partner with confidence and expression. In pairs, record your reading and play it back. Your partner can suggest further ways to improve your reading.

Check your progress

Good progress »
I can read a story with increasing confidence.

Excellent progress »»
I can read a story with confidence and expression.

Check your progress

Good progress »»

- ☐ I can use some strategies to help me read difficult words.
- ☐ I can listen to a story and work out what some difficult words mean.
- ☐ I can read a story with increasing confidence.

Excellent progress »»»

- ☐ I can use a range of strategies to help me read with confidence.
- ☐ I can read independently and work out how to say unfamiliar words.
- ☐ I can read a story with confidence and expression.

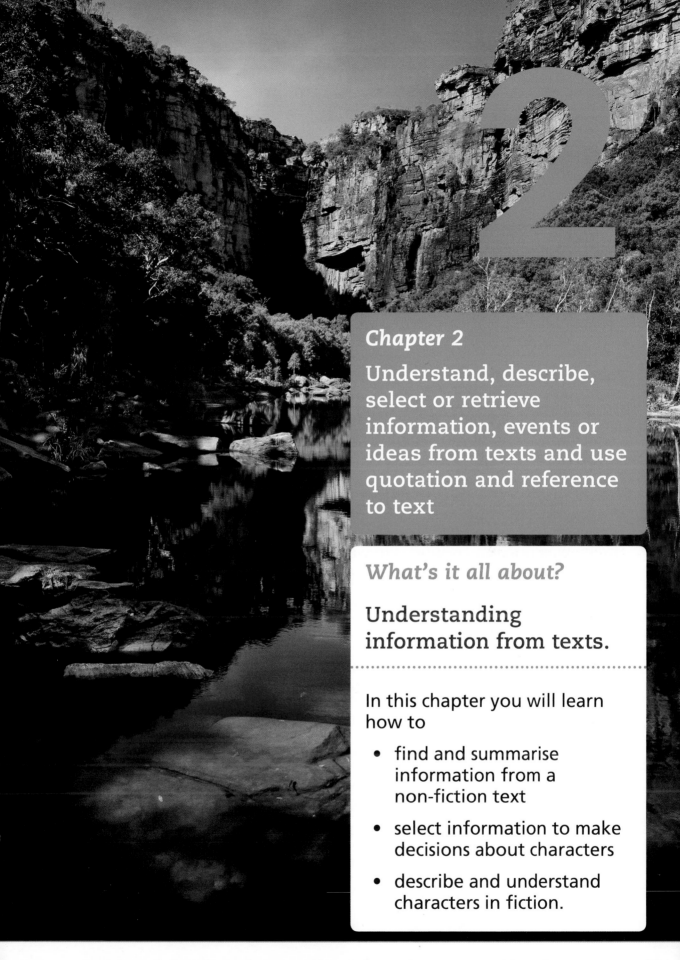

Chapter 2

Understand, describe, select or retrieve information, events or ideas from texts and use quotation and reference to text

What's it all about?

Understanding information from texts.

In this chapter you will learn how to

- find and summarise information from a non-fiction text

- select information to make decisions about characters

- describe and understand characters in fiction.

Find and summarise information from a non-fiction text

Getting you thinking

Non-fiction means that the people in the book really lived and the events in the book really happened. Your teacher will read you the text below:

Australia, 1860

In those days nobody knew what was in the middle of Australia. There might be a great lake or unknown cities. There might be more strange animals to find. Somebody had to explore Australia by walking from the South to the North. This man was Robert Burke.

Burke was born in Ireland. He was in the army there and then he joined the police. Later, he left Ireland and moved to a city called Melbourne, in Australia. He became a policeman there.

Burke liked police work. But sometimes it was boring. He wanted to do more with his life. Exploring Australia might bring him fame and fortune.

But there was a problem. Exploring a new country takes a lot of skill. You have to be ready when things go wrong. You have to have a plan. You have to know what to take and what to leave behind. Burke had never explored anywhere before. He knew nothing about leading a team.

The Great Trek by James Rigg

1 Answer these questions about the text. Look for key words in the questions to help you find the answers.

a) Where was Burke born?

b) What was his first job?

c) What was his second job?

d) What didn't he like about his second job?

e) Why did he want to explore Australia?

f) Why was Burke not the best person to explore Australia?

How does it work?

You will have found key words such as 'where' and 'born' in the questions to help you find the answers.

In the next activity, you will *summarise* the text. This means include only the most important points. A summary must be shorter than the original text and should not include details.

Now you try it

2 Look at the first paragraph. With a partner, work out how you could summarise it in one sentence.

3 Now, with your partner, write a summary for each of the other paragraphs. Try to use only one sentence for each summary.

Apply your skills

This text contains more information about
Robert Burke. Read it in small groups:

> He made mistakes. The group began to make good progress. But
> the land was as dry as a bone. Another explorer, Wills, was worried
> they'd run out of water. But Burke was in too much of a rush to
> worry. He didn't even stop at water holes. It might slow him down.
> If they spotted one in the afternoon he'd just pass by. He made his
> team march 16 hours a day. It didn't matter how thirsty they got.
>
> But in the end even Burke had to stop for water. They'd reached
> some mountains. Between the mountains were deep valleys. In the
> valleys were dark pools of good water. They filled their water bags.
> If they hadn't come across the pools, they'd have died of thirst.

4 Work in small groups to answer these questions:

a) Jot down the mistakes you think Burke made.

b) Summarise the mistakes in one sentence.

c) Work out why the explorers were lucky.

5 Hot seating: choose one member of your group to be Robert Burke. Ask him questions about his leadership.

Here are some questions you could use:

- Why did you think you would make a good explorer?

- What have you done in the past to make you a good team leader?

- Why didn't you stop at water holes to allow the team to refill their water bags?

Now think of your own questions to ask Burke.

Check your progress

Good progress 》》

I can find information in a non-fiction text.

Excellent progress 》》

I can find and summarise information in a non-fiction text.

Select information to make decisions about characters

Read these four character descriptions:

Jason Smart
Tall and thin. Full of fun, but gets into trouble quickly. Tries to talk himself out of trouble. A known pickpocket, but never caught.

Jeremy Brading
Average height, a bit overweight. Quiet – likes to spend time on the computer. Is loyal to his friends, very reliable. Enjoys football – usually plays in goal.

Emma Harman
Blonde, lively and talkative. Enjoys listening to hip hop. Has an eye for the boys, but not very loyal. Silly in class.

Shelley Collit
Enjoys looking after small children. Loves her two pet dogs, her guinea pig and her baby rabbit. Likes to hang out with a small group of friends. Tries her best with school work.

1 Now answer these questions:

    a) Which character likes animals?

    b) Which character likes music?

    c) Which description does not include anything about the character's appearance?

2 Show your partner which parts of the text helped you answer each question.

How does it work?

Looking for key words in the questions will help you find the answers. For example, the word 'animals' in the first question will mean you scan each description looking for something about animals.

Now you try it

3 Answer these questions. Find information from the text to back up what you say:

    a) Which of the four characters would you *like* as a friend? Why?

    b) Which of the four characters would you *not like* as a friend? Why?

Apply your skills

4 With a partner, discuss how you make decisions about characters in books, plays and films. Is it the way they look, what they say or what they do? Is it what other characters think and say about them?

Check your progress

Good progress >>>
I can find information from the text about characters.

Excellent progress >>>
I can form opinions about characters, using the text to back up my ideas.

Describe and understand characters in fiction

This extract is from a fiction story. The writer made the story up, which is why it is called fiction. Your teacher will read the story.

I hate school trips. I was only going on this one to keep my mother happy. 'Try not to get into bother this time,' she said as I was leaving. 'Make me proud for once.'

I always try to make my mother proud! I'm not bad, just unlucky. When something happens, I'm there, and I get the blame.

Somebody kicked the football through the school window. We were all playing football; I just happened to be the one who kicked the ball. See what I mean? Unlucky.

And when the PE teacher told me to throw away my chewing gum, how was I to know it would land in Chelsea's hair? Unlucky, I tell you.

Now I was on a final warning. 'Behave, or else, MacDuff!' the teacher, Mr Hoss, had told me.

'This school trip is your last chance!'

Last Chance MacDuff, that's me.

Point Danger by Catherine MacPhail

1 With a partner, re-read the text very carefully. Then answer these questions about Mark MacDuff:

a) What does Macduff's mother think about him?

b) What two things has MacDuff done to get him into trouble?

c) What is he told about his behaviour and the school trip?

d) What does MacDuff think about himself and luck?

e) Do you think he is right?

How does it work?

You should work out that MacDuff is often in trouble. He thinks he is just unlucky, but he might be wrong.

Now you try it

In the next extract, MacDuff is on a ferry as part of the school trip:

> No wonder I was standing alone. The rest of the class didn't like me, and I don't like them. For a start, there were Tom and Alex. They looked down their noses at me. You know their kind. Teacher's pets and all that. They shuffled away from me as if I had B.O.
>
> Then there was Gary Bond. He was never far away from Tom and Alex, always doing what they told him. They said, 'Jump', and Gary asked, 'How high?'

2 **a)** What does MacDuff think about Tom and Alex?

b) What does he think about Gary Bond?

c) Why do you think Tom and Alex stay away from MacDuff?

3 How would you describe the characters below?

- Gary Bond

- Mr Hoss

- MacDuff (Can you believe everything he says?)

4 How has the writer made the characters different from one another?

- Is it what they do and say?

- Is it what MacDuff tells us about them?

Discuss your ideas in small groups.

Check your progress

Good progress ⟫

I can describe characters in a text.

Excellent progress ⟫

I can understand how a writer develops characters in a text.

Check your progress

Good progress

☐ I can find information in a non-fiction text.

☐ I can find information from the text about characters.

☐ I can describe characters in a text.

Excellent progress

☐ I can find and summarise information in a non-fiction text.

☐ I can form opinions about characters, using the text to back up my ideas.

☐ I can understand how a writer develops characters in a text.

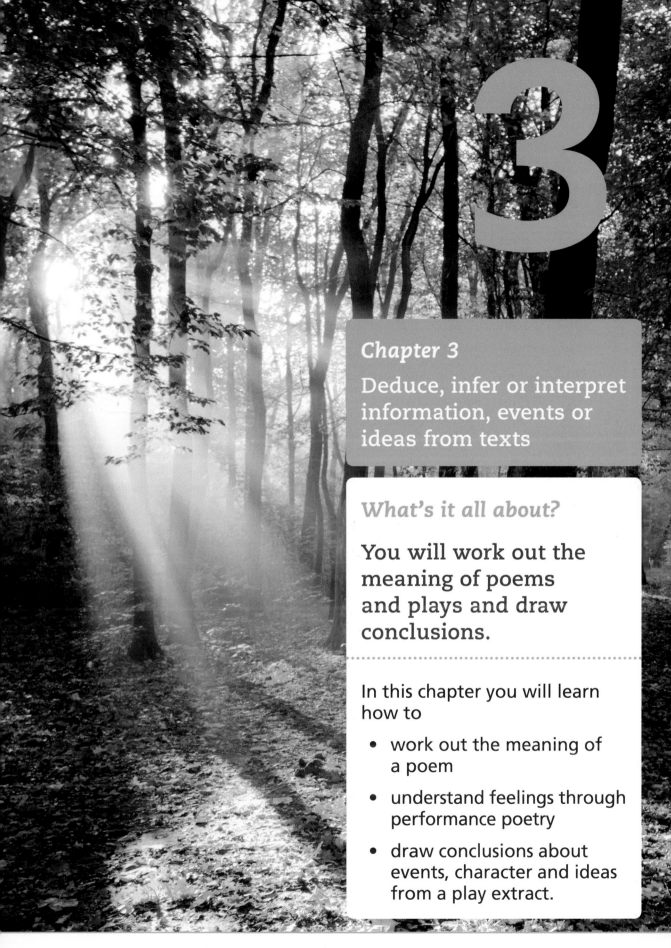

3

Chapter 3
Deduce, infer or interpret information, events or ideas from texts

What's it all about?

You will work out the meaning of poems and plays and draw conclusions.

In this chapter you will learn how to

- work out the meaning of a poem

- understand feelings through performance poetry

- draw conclusions about events, character and ideas from a play extract.

Work out the meaning of a poem

Getting you thinking

Your teacher will read the first four verses of this poem. In small groups, you can then read small sections to each other:

1   Salford Road, Salford Road,
    Is the place where I was born,
    With a green front gate, a red brick wall
    And **hydrangeas** round a lawn.

2   Salford Road, Salford Road,
    Is the road where we would play
    Where the sky lay over the roof tops
    Like a friend who'd come to stay.

3   The Gardeners lived at fifty-five,
    The Lunds with the willow tree,
    Mr Pool with the flag and the garden pond
    And the Harndens at fifty-three.

4   There was riding bikes and laughing
    Till we couldn't laugh any more,
    And **bilberries** picked on the hillside
    And picnics on the shore.

1 Now, with a partner, work out what these four verses are about.

Glossary

hydrangeas: plants with blue or pink flowers

bilberries: dark blue berries

How does it work?

This poem is mysterious. A mystery poem is not going to *tell* you what is happening. Like a detective, you have to work out what's going on from the clues in the text.

Now you try it

Your teacher will now read the next three verses to you.

5 I lay in bed when I was four
 As the sunlight turned to grey
 And heard the train through my pillow
 And the seagulls far away.

6 And I rose to look out of my window
 For I knew that someone was there
 And a man stood sad as nevermore
 And didn't see me there.

7 And when I stand in Salford Road
 And think of the boy who was me
 I feel that from one of the windows
 Someone is looking at me.

2 Who do you think the man who stood 'as sad as nevermore' is?

3 Why do you think the man didn't see the little boy?

4 Re-read verse 7. The poet is now standing and looking up at the window. He feels that someone is looking down at him. Who do you think is looking down at him?

Apply your skills

Now your teacher will read the final verses of the poem to you:

8 My friends walked out one Summer day,
   Walked singing down the lane,
   My friends walked into a wood called Time
   And never came out again.

9 We live in a land called Gone-Today
   That's made of bricks and straw
   But Salford Road runs through my head
   To a land called Evermore.

From *Salford Road* by Gareth Owen

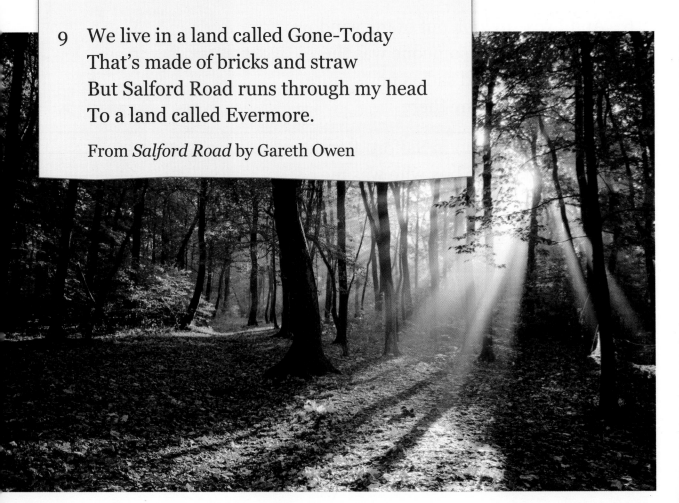

5 Re-read verse 8. Did the poet's friends really disappear in a wood? What do you think really happened? Which word gives you a clue?

6 Look again at verse 9. Can you work out the meaning of this verse?

- What is this land called Evermore? Is it a real place?

- As a clue, think of your past. What happens to your past thoughts and experiences? What do they become?

7 Which of these adjectives best describes this poem? (If you don't know the meanings of these words, look them up in a dictionary.)

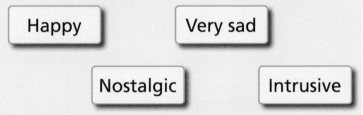

Happy   Very sad

Nostalgic   Intrusive

Can you think of any other adjectives to describe the mood of the poem?

Check your progress

Good progress 〉〉〉
I can understand some of the ideas in the poem.

Excellent progress 〉〉〉
I can understand the meaning and describe the mood of the poem.

Understand feelings through performance poetry

Listen to the poem as your teacher reads it to you:

Conversation Piece

Late again Blenkinsop?
What's the excuse this time?
Not my fault sir.
Whose fault is it then?
5 *Grandma's sir.*
Grandma's. What did she do?
She died sir.
Died?
She's seriously dead all right sir.
10 That makes four grandmothers this term
And all on PE days Blenkinsop.
I know. It's very upsetting sir.
How many grandmothers have you got Blenkinsop?
Grandmothers sir? None sir.
15 None?
All dead sir.
And what about yesterday Blenkinsop?
What about yesterday sir?
You missed maths.
20 *That was the dentist sir.*

Deduce, infer or interpret information, events or ideas from texts

The dentist died?
No sir. My teeth sir.
You missed the test Blenkinsop.
I'd been looking forward to it too sir.
25 Right, line up for PE.
Can't sir.
No such word as can't. Why can't you?
No kit sir.
Where is it?
30 *Home sir.*
What's it doing at home?
Not ironed sir.
Couldn't you iron it?
Can't do it sir.
35 Why not?
My hand sir.
Who usually does it?
Grandma sir.
Why couldn't she do it?
40 *Dead sir.*

by Gareth Owen

1 This poem is called 'Conversation Piece'.
Who do you think the conversation
is between?

How does it work?

This is a performance poem. The title,
'Conversation Piece', gives us a clue that it is
meant to be read aloud. Blenkinsop's words
are in italics. This helps to show who is talking.

When you come to read it in pairs, think about how each character is feeling at different points in the poem.

Now you try it

2 Look at lines 1–24:

a) How does the teacher feel at this point in the story?

b) What do you think Blenkinsop might be thinking?

3 Look at lines 25–40:

a) Who do you think wins the argument? Why?

b) Does Blenkinsop like or dislike PE? Can you work out the answer from the poem?

c) What words would you use to describe this poem?

4 If you were reading the teacher's lines, what tone of voice would you use? Would your tone change at any point?

5 Working in pairs, perform the poem.

If possible, record your performance. Then play back or watch it to see if you can improve it. Does performing and recording the poem help you understand it better?

6 You are now going to improvise (act out without writing it down first) your own performance poem.

Imagine Blenkinsop goes to a skatepark after school. This makes him late for tea and he needs excuses. Working in pairs, one of you can be his mum or dad and one can be Blenkinsop. As Blenkinsop is at home, you will need to think of a first name for him.

Example:
Late again, Jamie Blenkinsop?

Not that late, mum.

Your tea is ruined. What's your excuse?

Sorry, mum. It wasn't my fault...

Check your progress

Good progress 〉〉〉
I can understand the meaning of the poem.

Excellent progress 〉〉〉
I can understand the meaning and the tone of the poem.

Draw conclusions about events, character and ideas from a play extract

Getting you thinking

In groups of four, read the play extract and act it out:

Bad

(*A block of flats. Ethan is hoping to escape from a gang, who are searching for him.*)

ETHAN   (*to himself*) Got to lay low. Wait 'till they get bored. Wait 'till they've gone. (*sniggers*) They won't have any heat-seeking device...will they?

GEORGE   (*behind Ethan*) Boo!

LUCAS   Got you!

ETHAN   (*standing up*) W... what do you want? Let me go!

LUCAS   (*mimics Ethan*) Let me go, let me go, let me go!

AIDEN   (*in front of Ethan, almost nose to nose*) We want you to do something for us!

(*George and Lucas snigger.*)

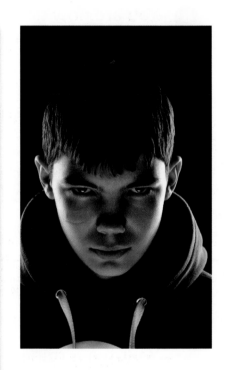

ETHAN   (*shakily*) What? W... what do you want me to do?

AIDEN   Ah, now that's a little secret we ain't going to tell you until we're outta this place.

LUCAS   Yeah, we'll all have some fun!

GEORGE   (*laughs*) We're due for some entertainment.

AIDEN   We'll get him to do the car tonight.

LUCAS   (*surprised*) No, we can't let him do that. It's too dangerous.

AIDEN   Shut up, Lucas. Who runs this show? Me or you?

LUCAS   But...

AIDEN   (*interrupting*) SHUT IT!

1 In pairs, talk about these questions. Jot down your answers:

a) Where does the play take place?

b) What are Ethan's thoughts at the start of the play?

c) How does he feel when he's caught?

d) Who is the gang leader? How do we know?

e) What might happen next in the play?

How does it work?

Playwrights tell us more about characters by including information about how they feel, think and act. They put this information in brackets before the characters speak.

2 Choose one character from the play and look more closely at what he says and does. What does this tell you about his personality?

a) What conclusions can you draw about the character you have chosen? Think about

- what he does
- what he says
- how he says it
- how he treats others.

You might want to use some words from the word bank below.

bully frightened gang

threaten dangerous

b) What might the character you have chosen go on to do?

Apply your skills

3 Why do you think the title of the play is *Bad*?

4 The ideas in a play are sometimes called its *themes*. What do you think the themes of this play are?

Check your progress

Good progress

I can understand what is happening in the play.

Excellent progress

I can draw conclusions about events, character and ideas in the play.

Check your progress

- I can understand some of the ideas in a poem.
- I can understand the meaning of a poem.
- I can understand what is happening in a play.

- I can understand the meaning and describe the mood of a poem.
- I can understand the meaning and the tone of a poem.
- I can draw conclusions about events, characters and ideas in a play.

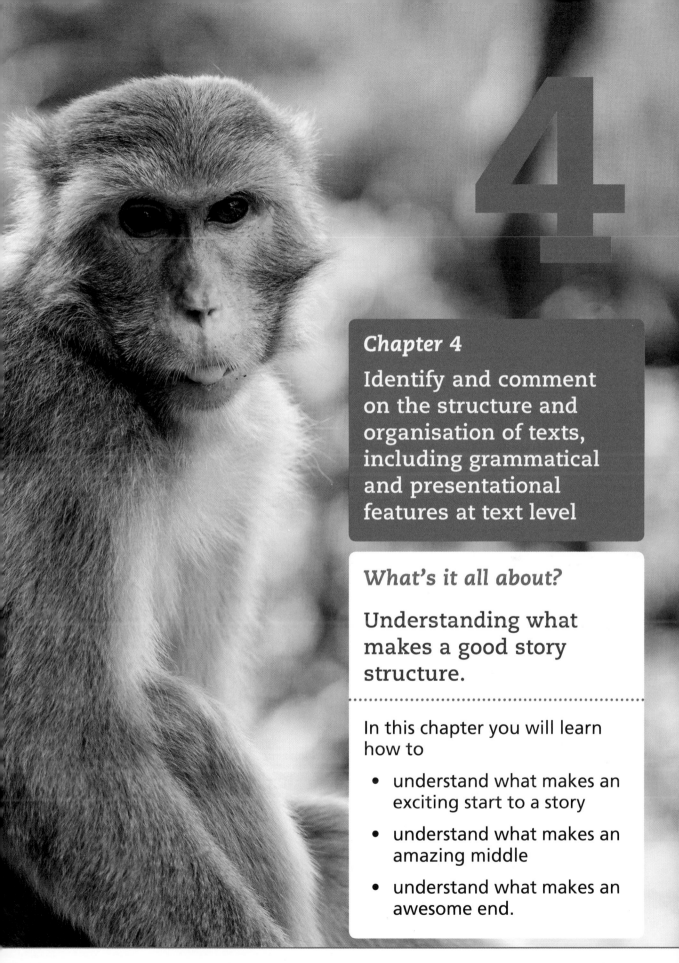

Chapter 4

Identify and comment on the structure and organisation of texts, including grammatical and presentational features at text level

What's it all about?

Understanding what makes a good story structure.

In this chapter you will learn how to

- understand what makes an exciting start to a story
- understand what makes an amazing middle
- understand what makes an awesome end.

Understand what makes an exciting start to a story

Getting you thinking

1 Read the five story starts below. Then put them in order from the one you think is most exciting to the one you think is least exciting. Discuss your reasons with a partner:

I remember the day Skink arrived like it only just happened. I remember it so well 'cos it was the day that things changed forever.

Mrs MacDonald was over 70, but full of great ideas. She wanted to invent a time machine but never quite got started. Until last week...

Fire! The whole building was ablaze. I had to get out and get out fast. The smoke was choking me and I broke a window so I could breathe.

I first met Jack when he arrived for football training. Straight away, I knew he was different.

'Look!' my sister screamed. 'There's a shape in the mist! It's...the ghost of a girl...'

2 Do the five story starts have anything in common?

How does it work?

Writers often use the start of a story to 'hook' the reader in. The start might be exciting or different in some way, so the reader will want to read on. The writer often sets the scene quickly and introduces the characters in more detail later.

Now you try it

The first story start on page 42 is from a book called *The Mighty Skink*. Your teacher will read the rest of the story opening to you.

I remember the day Skink arrived like it only just happened. I remember it so well 'cos it was the day that things changed forever.

I spent the morning just swinging around the outer branches of the Big Tree. It was my most favourite spot in the whole wide world. Every once in a while I let out this great big whoop, like this:

WHOOOOOOOOOO-UP! WHOOOOOOOO-UP!

It's not easy to get a whoop just right, you know. You've got to start it right deep down in your belly, then kind of build it up in your chest, so it gets louder and louder, until it rises at the end for the final *-UP!* bit.

Don't go thinking I was up there just to practise my whooping noises though. I wanted to get some good thinking done, and you couldn't do *that* down on the ground with the rest of the Tribe all chattering around you and making a din. That's why the Big Tree was really good – you could scoot up it and almost feel like you were on your own. But the best bit was, it had this great view of what was outside our Enclosure. What I'd do, I'd climb up to my branch and spend hours just looking out across The Fence.

Chim, who was my best friend – even though I'd never tell him that in a million years – he always said that I spent too much time thinking. He said that I'd wear my brain out with thinking too much, and I'd end up this crazy old monkey that couldn't even unzip a banana for myself. Hah!

The Mighty Skink by Paul Shipton

3 Answer these questions about the opening of *The Mighty Skink*:

a) What kind of animal is telling the story? How do you know?

b) How does the first paragraph 'hook' the reader in?

c) Do you think the story is funny? Pick out some funny words or phrases.

d) What do you think the rest of the story might be about?

4 The writer has used some interesting words to set the scene and describe the characters:

a) Where do you think the story is set? Which words tell you this?

b) Why do you think the nouns 'Enclosure' and 'The Fence' have capital letters?

c) Can you find an interesting verb (action word) that describes how the animals behave?

5 With a partner, list the reasons why the start to *The Mighty Skink* might make you want to read on.

Apply your skills

6 Imagine *The Mighty Skink* has won a prize for an exciting start to a book. You are the prize giver and you are writing a speech for the award ceremony. In your speech you should say why the book has won the award.

Check your progress

Good progress 》》

I can recognise an exciting start to a story.

Excellent progress 》》

I can work out what makes an exciting start to a story and give reasons for why I like it.

Understand what makes an amazing middle

Read the extract below to a partner. It is from the middle of a story.

Amelia's Nightmare

Amelia sat in the café. She sipped her coffee and wondered what had happened to her dad. She'd spent ages trying to find him. She'd got nowhere. The waiter came up to her and told her to go. He needed to close the café. She wanted to phone her friends, to tell them she was safe. She looked at her mobile, but the battery was very low. She didn't like the look in the waiter's eyes. She knew she had to leave. She picked up her bag and walked towards the door. Outside, it was raining. This was going to be a long night. 'I know all about your dad,' said the waiter. Amelia shivered. He'd read her thoughts.

1 What is Amelia's problem at the start of this extract?

2 There is a new problem to keep the reader interested by the end of the extract. What is it?

How does it work?

The middle of a story usually includes a problem. The problem keeps the reader hooked – they want to know how the character(s) will solve the problem.

Writers also keep the reader hooked by using interesting descriptions of people and places.

Now you try it

Your teacher will read the following extract to you. It is another version of *Amelia's Nightmare*.

Amelia sat in the café. She was tired and her head ached. She had to find her dad. She needed to find clues from somewhere.

The waiter smiled at her, shrugging his shoulders. 'Time to go, love. I'm shutting up in a few moments,' he said.

He smiled, but there was something about him she didn't like. She distrusted him. His smile didn't seem real.

She glanced at her mobile, gripped in her cold hands. The battery was low. She couldn't phone her friends. She couldn't let them know where she was or how she was feeling.

Amelia stood up from the table. She adjusted her rucksack and walked towards the battered café door.

By now the rain was hammering on the roof. This was going to be a long night.

'I know all about your dad,' hissed the waiter.

Amelia shivered. He'd read her thoughts.

3 Describe the character of the waiter to your partner. Think about the following questions:

- What does the word 'hissed' suggest about him?

- What do Amelia's thoughts and the description of him suggest?

- What does Amelia's reaction ('Amelia shivered') suggest about the way he makes her feel?

4   Which extract did you like best and why?

- Which includes more description?

- Which tells us more?

- Do you prefer shorter paragraphs?

- Why might shorter paragraphs work better?

Write one or two sentences saying why one was better than the other and which made the best 'middle' of a story.

Check your progress

Good progress

I can understand that the middle of a story usually contains a problem.

Excellent progress

I can understand that the middle of a story usually contains a problem and also that structure and description can improve a story.

Understand what makes an awesome end

Getting you thinking

What could happen next in *Amelia's Nightmare*? Here are some ideas for the end:

- Amelia's dad works for a bank. A gang was trying to force him to rob the bank.

- The waiter tells Amelia that the gang is holding her dad prisoner in a nearby hut.

- Amelia texts her friend Joel before the battery on her phone runs out.

- Joel tells the police, who surround the hut.

- The police charge the hut. Amelia's dad is rescued and Joel is a hero.

1 What do you think about these ideas for the end of *Amelia's Nightmare*? Have all the problems been solved?

How does it work?

The ending of a story is important. The problem or problems that came up in the middle of the story are usually solved at the end.

Now you try it

2 With a partner, talk about the structure and organisation of a story you know well. Does it work? Is it exciting? Is there a problem in the middle of the story that is solved by the end?

3 See if you can come up with an alternative ending for *Amelia's Nightmare* or a story you know. Use bullet points for three to five different events that could happen in the story you have chosen. The ideas should help you write an awesome end.

Apply your skills

4 Read your ideas for the end of a story to each other. Which ideas would make the best story end? Give reasons for your answer. If possible, act out the best story ending.

Check your progress

Good progress »
I can understand that the problem in a story is usually solved at the end.

Excellent progress »»
I can understand that the problem in a story is usually solved at the end and can give reasons for why I like a story end.

Check your progress

Good progress 〉〉

- ☐ I can recognise an exciting start to a story.
- ☐ I can understand that the middle of a story usually contains a problem.
- ☐ I can understand that the problem in a story is usually solved at the end.

Excellent progress 〉〉〉

- ☐ I can work out what makes an exciting start to a story and give reasons for why I like it.
- ☐ I can understand that the middle of a story usually contains a problem and also that structure and description can improve a story.
- ☐ I can understand that the problem in a story is usually solved at the end and can give reasons for why I like a story end.

5

Chapter 5

Explain and comment on writers' use of language, including grammatical and literary features at word and sentence level

What's it all about?

The words a writer chooses can make a big difference to the text.

In this chapter you will learn how to

- understand and comment on the writer's use of language in a traditional tale

- understand and comment on the writer's use of language in a modern tale.

Understand and comment on the writer's use of language in a traditional tale

Your teacher will read this traditional fairy tale to you.

Some of the words are underlined. You will be working with those words in a later activity.

The Princess and the Frog

Once upon a time there lived a king. He had a beautiful daughter. They lived in a big castle. Near the castle there was a dark forest. In the forest, under an old lime tree, was a deep well. The king's daughter went near the well when she was bored. She took a ball with her and she played throw and catch. She played throw and catch on her own.

One day the ball fell into the well. The ball sank in the water. The king's daughter was so sad that she cried. Then something suddenly spoke from the well.

'What's the matter, king's daughter? Why are you crying?'

When the princess looked around, all she could see was a frog. Its big, ugly head popped from the water.

'I'm crying because my ball has fallen into the well,' <u>sobbed</u> the princess.

The frog croaked.

'What will you give me if I find your ball at the bottom of the well?'

The princess thought carefully.

'You can have anything I own. <u>Pearls</u>, <u>jewels</u>, even my <u>golden crown</u>.

The frog thought for a moment and answered, 'I don't care for your pearls, jewels or your golden crown. I just want to be your friend.'

The princess agreed and the frog found her ball. The princess grabbed the ball and ran off. She did not trust a talking frog and she did not want to be friends with something so ugly. She ran all the way to the king, who was counting money in the palace counting room.

The princess told her father everything. The king told her that she had to keep her promise. She hated the ugly, cold frog and she did not want to see it again. The king grew angry.

'The frog helped you when you were in trouble. You must not hate him now.'

The princess found the frog and carried it to her room. She wanted to lie down and rest. The frog looked at her with his big <u>bulging</u> eyes.

'Let me lie next to you,' he <u>croaked</u>. 'I'm tired too.'

The princess grew angry. She picked the frog up and threw him against the wall.

'Now be quiet, you horrible little frog,' she cried.

When she looked down, the frog had turned into a handsome prince.

'I was <u>bewitched</u> and turned into a frog by a wicked witch. I had to remain a frog until a princess took me into her room.'

The prince and princess married and lived happily ever after.

1 In pairs, read the fairy tale again. What words and phrases tell us this is a fairy tale?

2 Look at the different kinds of words the writer has used. Find an example of

   a) a noun (a person, place or thing)

   b) a verb (an action word)

   c) an adjective (a describing word)

   d) an adverb (a word that tells us more about a verb or adjective and often ends in *ly*).

How does it work?

Traditional fairy tales often start with 'Once upon a time' and end with 'lived happily ever after'. They often have characters such as princesses and talking animals, and settings such as a magical forest or castle.

The writer of 'The Princess and the Frog' has also chosen some interesting verbs, adjectives and nouns. Look at the words underlined in the story. For example:

- using the verb 'croak' instead of 'say' tells us how the frog speaks

- using the adjective 'bulging' gives us the idea that the frog's eyes were almost popping out of his head

- the nouns 'pearls' and 'jewels' and the phrase 'golden crown' make the princess sound rich.

Now you try it

3 Working in pairs, write down as many titles of folk and fairy stories as you can think of.

4 Now write down as many typical characters and objects from fairy stories as you can think of.

Wherever you can, add an adjective to give more information.

Examples: A *handsome* prince
              A *wicked* queen
              A *magic* castle

Apply your skills

5 Working in pairs, look at the words in the table and think of an alternative word for each. Decide which words you think work best – the writer's word or your alternative. The first one has been done for you.

Word choice	Alternatives	Which works best?
Sobbed	Cried	Sobbed works best because the writer has used the word cried already.
Croaked		
Grabbed		
Bulging		
Bewitched		

Top tip

Use a thesaurus to help you find a good alternative word.

Check your progress

Good progress 》》

I can recognise the words and phrases used in a traditional tale.

Excellent progress 》》

I can comment on the writer's choice of language in a traditional tale.

Understand and comment on the writer's use of language in a modern tale

Getting you thinking

Your teacher will read the story below to you. Notice how the writer makes different word and phrase choices for a modern tale:

The Princess and the Frog
(A modern version)

Not long ago there lived a king. He had a daughter who was a spoilt brat. They lived in a luxury mansion and she had everything she needed – except a friend. She'd fallen out with all her friends.

She used to play with a big ball near her outdoor swimming pool. She did this because she was bored and lonely and had no friends.

One day the ball fell into the pool and floated away. Because she was spoilt, the princess began to cry.

She only stopped crying when she heard somebody asking her what was wrong.

When the princess wiped her eyes, she noticed a big ugly frog with bulging eyes.

'I'm crying because my ball has floated to the middle of the pool. Now I'm speaking to a talking frog. I must be going mad!'

The princess sobbed even more. She offered the frog all she owned, including her pearls, jewels and golden crown. The stupid, ugly frog didn't want anything of value; he just wanted to go wherever she went. The princess readily agreed. She knew she could outrun a frog!

'Yeah, whatever!' she said.

'Cool,' croaked the frog and he swam to the ball.

The princess grabbed the ball and ran.

'Wait for me,' said the frog.

The princess gave a cruel laugh.

'No way! I don't trust a talking frog. I'm not being friends with anything so ugly. It'd ruin my image. And don't think I'm going to kiss you. Yuck!'

The princess ran back to the mansion and told her dad everything. He was angry. He told his daughter that the frog had helped her when she was in trouble, so she should help the frog now. The princess turned pale.

'Dream on, Dad. I'm not being friends with a horrid, ugly frog.'

The king was angry. He told his daughter she'd do as she was told or he'd banish her from the country. She'd have nowhere to go. She'd become poor. She'd have to work for a living!

The princess quickly found the frog and took it to her room. She lay on her bed and threw the frog against the mansion wall.

'Now be quiet forever, you horrid lump of hopping jelly,' she cried. 'Hope I've killed you!'

A prince stood up. 'Well, you've given me a few bruises,' he said.

The princess eyed the prince up and down. He wasn't bad-looking. He'd do! They married in haste and the prince soon regretted marrying the spoilt princess. She nagged him to an early death.

1 How are the start and ending in the modern tale different from those in the traditional tale?

How does it work?

The author uses some words and phrases to give the tale a modern feel, for example 'Cool', 'Dream on' and 'horrid lump of hopping jelly'. This version also shows us that the princess is spoilt. When her dad tells her he'd banish her, she loses her temper and tries to kill the frog. The ending is different too – it isn't a 'happy ever after' fairy tale. The prince is nagged to death!

Now you try it

2 Pick out other words and phrases that the author has chosen to make the story seem modern.

3 Are there any words or phrases that the writer has used that you particularly like? Are there any that you don't like? Give reasons for your answers.

Apply your skills

4 Choose a fairy story or folk tale and make a plan of how you would turn it into a modern story. For example:

Traditional story: *Snow White*	My modern version: *Ebony Black*
Beginning: Once upon a time in a faraway kingdom…	**Beginning**: It happened in a country so far away it would take you at least a day to get there by plane…
Main events: 1 There is a princess called Snow White. 2 She has a jealous stepmother who has a magic mirror.	**Main events:** 1 There is a celebrity wannabe called Ebony Black. 2 She has a jealous stepmother who has a magic computer.

5 Use your plan to write the opening of your story and then ask a partner to read it. Do they like your choice of modern words and phrases? Is there anything they would change?

Check your progress

Check your progress

Good progress 〉〉

- ☐ I can recognise the words and phrases used in a traditional tale.
- ☐ I can identify the writer's choice of language in a modern tale.

Excellent progress 〉〉〉

- ☐ I can comment on the writer's choice of language in a traditional tale.
- ☐ I can comment on the writer's choice of language in a modern tale.

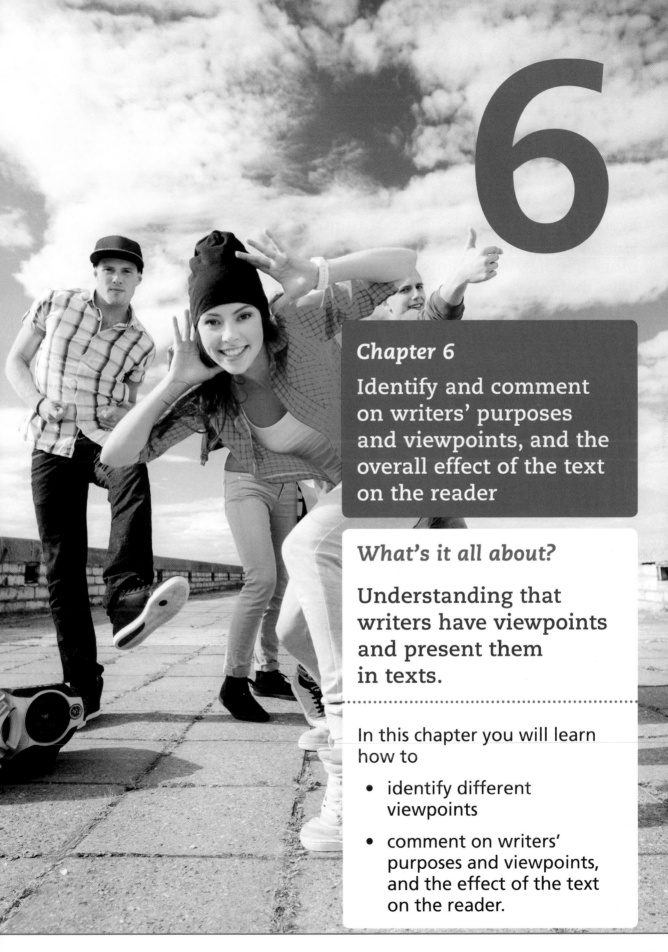

6

Chapter 6

Identify and comment on writers' purposes and viewpoints, and the overall effect of the text on the reader

What's it all about?

Understanding that writers have viewpoints and present them in texts.

In this chapter you will learn how to

- identify different viewpoints

- comment on writers' purposes and viewpoints, and the effect of the text on the reader.

Identify different viewpoints

Getting you thinking

Everyone has a viewpoint about things. Some people may want to disagree with other people's viewpoints because they have their own.

With a partner, read a viewpoint from each of the following pairs:

> I think Liverpool is the best football club in Britain.

Nathan

> No way. Manchester United is the best. They've won the league title more times than any other club.

Joanne

> I love English! The lessons are so interesting.

Aisha

> What a joke! All we do is read or write. Maths is far more fun.

Wayne

1 Some people have given a reason for their point of view and others have not. Can you identify which people have given a reason?

How does it work?

We are all different and think differently about things. We have viewpoints that others may agree or disagree with. Often you will need to recognise a writer's viewpoint in a text.

Now you try it

2 Look at the four statements below. For each one, write down a different viewpoint, giving a reason for that viewpoint.

> Children should be allowed on the computer for as long as they like because it helps them to learn.

> All dog owners should keep their dogs on a lead in case the dog attacks someone.

> Football managers shouldn't be sacked because it's the players' fault if a team is doing badly.

> Bullies should be separated from other pupils so they learn not to bully.

Apply your skills

3 Which of these kinds of texts do you think might include the writer's viewpoint? Discuss your ideas in a small group:

- A letter to a friend
- A manual for a washing machine
- A fairytale
- A newspaper article about a film.

Check your progress

Good progress 》》
I can recognise a viewpoint.

Excellent progress 》》
I can recognise a viewpoint and understand what kinds of texts include viewpoints.

Comment on writers' purposes and viewpoints, and the effect of the text on the reader

Read this letter:

Dear Head Teacher,

All teenagers are horrible, but your students are worse than any I have ever seen. They are an absolute disgrace!

Your students wear their uniform but it looks a mess. Their ties are undone and their shoes need a good clean. In my view you should check the state of their uniforms. If the uniforms are scruffy they should all be sent home.

I demand you reply to this letter.

Yours sincerely,

Desmond Worldwise

1 Summarise the viewpoint given in this letter.

2 Look at the letter again. What words or phrases has Desmond Worldwise used to express his viewpoint forcefully?

How does it work?

You can see that some people express their opinions forcefully. Desmond Worldwise has used strong words such as 'disgrace' and 'demand.'

Now you try it

Read the speech Sonya Harper gave to parents at her school's speech day:

> I'm a Year 9 student. Most people hate sport at our school.
>
> I wrote out a survey and asked everyone what they'd like to do to keep healthy. Street dancing came out tops!
>
> The whole thing has taken off. Some sixth-formers run the sessions and they're really popular!
>
> Please support our efforts to keep fit by sponsoring our street dancing. After all, you want your kids to stay fit and healthy, don't you?

3 How does this letter make you feel as a reader? Discuss your ideas with a partner.

Apply your skills

4 Look at the two letters:

a) Which do you think is better at persuading the reader? Why?

b) List any examples of words or phrases that persuade you the most.

Check your progress

Good progress »
I can recognise a writer's viewpoint and purpose.

Excellent progress »»
I can recognise a viewpoint and comment on its effect on the reader.

Check your progress

Good progress

- [ ] I can recognise a viewpoint.
- [ ] I can recognise a writer's viewpoint and purpose.

Excellent progress

- [ ] I can recognise a viewpoint and understand what kinds of texts include viewpoints.
- [ ] I can recognise a viewpoint and comment on its effect on the reader.

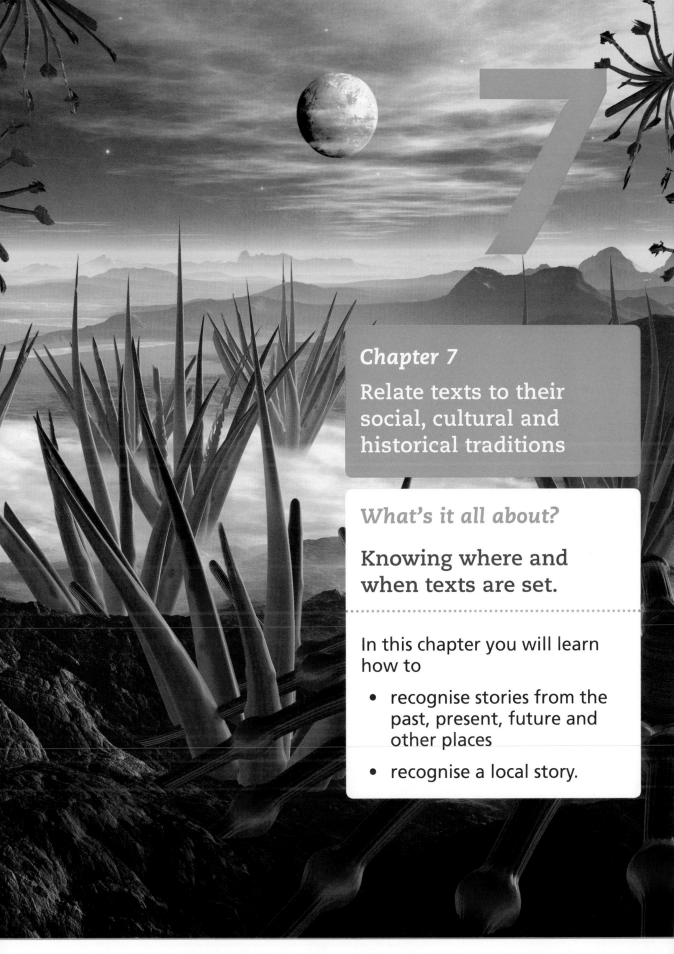

Chapter 7

Relate texts to their social, cultural and historical traditions

What's it all about?

Knowing where and when texts are set.

In this chapter you will learn how to

- recognise stories from the past, present, future and other places
- recognise a local story.

Recognise stories from the past, present, future and other places

Getting you thinking

1 Look at the following book covers. In small groups, decide which stories are set

- in the past
- in the present
- in the future
- in another country
- on another planet.

Make a table like the one below and fill it out.

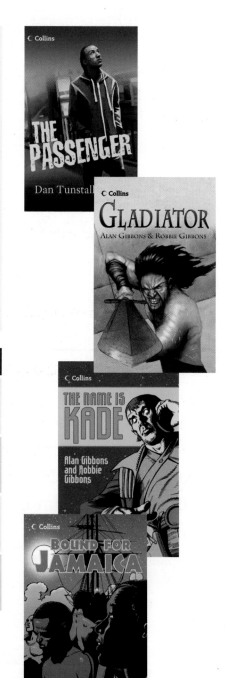

Book	Setting
The Passenger	
Gladiator	
The Name is Kade	
Bound for Jamaica	

The title and picture on the cover often give clues about when or where a story is set. For example, what does the title *Bound for Jamaica* tell you about the setting and what might happen in the story?

Now you try it

Now read these story extracts. As you are reading, try and work out when and where each of these stories is set:

- Is it in the past, present or future?

- Is it in another country?

Like the wind through the trees before the rain, we always knew when the story was coming. He would wait for a silence around the fire, lean forward warming his hands, and begin.

'In ancient time before any of you were even born, I was a young man. No cursed Roman soldier had yet set foot in this land of ours. We were not then a beaten people. We were wild perhaps, quarrelsome certainly, but we were our own people.'

In Ancient Time by Michael Morpurgo

2 **a)** When do you think this extract is set?

b) Which words and phrases tell you this?

This city was built on a swamp but you wouldn't be able to tell. We arrived on a hot day in June but didn't see a single mosquito.

There were wonderful buildings, which reminded me that St Petersburg was once Russia's capital city.

Boats bobbed gently on the river and car drivers beeped their horns in the rush-hour traffic.

Who could have guessed that even as we arrived in this beautiful and busy city, our lives were in danger.

Our Ordeal

3 **a)** Where and when do you think this extract is set?

b) Which words and phrases tell you this?

We had landed. The ground was rocky and covered in a strange mist. I thought I saw a blue creature moving amongst the weird, spiky plants. This creature could be dangerous, especially if it had taken a gun from the stockade...

The Planet X1

4 **a)** Where and when do you think this extract is set?

b) Which words and phrases tell you this?

Apply your skills

5 Now write a few sentences of a story, describing a setting from the past, present or future. Swap your work with a partner. Can your partner recognise where and when the story is set?

Check your progress

Good progress
I can work out if a story is set in the past, present or future.

Excellent progress
I can pick out words and phrases that tell me where and when the story is set.

Recognise a local story

Here is a ghost story from East Anglia. Your teacher will read this to you.

Glossary

sluss: water/rainwater

highlows: boots

We moved into an old farmhouse last month. The land is so flat here. It's in the Fenland and I can hear owls hoot at night. A pheasant sat on the lawn near my bedroom window. If I listen carefully, I can hear the wail of the sea and the cry of seagulls. There's the **sluss** running from the gutter on wet nights.

My brother and sisters are younger than me, so they got the upstairs bedrooms. Dad made me sleep in a room downstairs, next to the outhouse. I had to walk along a long, dusty corridor to get to it.

Dad had converted an old office into my bedroom. As soon as I saw my room, I was nervous. It sent shivers down my spine. The place was small and dark and gloomy.

Last night, I suddenly woke up. I could hear a noise. There was a small moan and a rustling sound. I could hear the squeak of the door handle as someone slowly turned it. My heart missed a beat.

I quickly turned on the bedroom light, jumped out of bed and opened the door, my **highlows** in my hands, ready to use as weapons.

There was nobody in the corridor. All I could hear was the wind whistling and moaning.

1 In groups, read the story again. Then answer the questions:

a) What does the story tell you about the landscape of East Anglia?

b) Two of the words are dialect words. This means they are only used in the local area. Can you spot which two words are the dialect words?

c) What tells you that this is a ghost story?

2 In your groups, discuss what makes a good ghost story.

Now you try it

3 Do you know any stories from your area? In small groups, try to think of a local story – you are going to tell one of these to the class. Something amazing might have happened to someone you know, or it could be a local ghost story you have heard about. Choose your story and jot it down in about six or seven bullet points.

Apply your skills

4 Retell your local story to the class. Remember to describe the local setting and use some local words where relevant.

Check your progress

Good progress ⟫

I can recognise some features of a local story.

Excellent progress ⟫⟫

I can recognise the features of a local story and can retell a local story.

Check your progress

Good progress ⟩⟩

- [ ] I can work out if a story is set in the past, present or future.
- [ ] I can recognise some features of a local story.

Excellent progress ⟩⟩⟩

- [ ] I can pick out words and phrases that tell me where and when a story is set.
- [ ] I can recognise the features of a local story and can retell a local story.

Teacher Guide

Securing basic literacy skills is a key priority for all children so they have the essential building blocks they need to become effective learners. The *Aiming for...* series supports the development of reading and writing skills in a structured yet engaging way whilst enabling teachers to effectively track the progress their students are making.

The activities in the books start by modelling the essential skills for students. This is followed by opportunities for them to practise and then demonstrate independently what they know and can do across each reading and writing strand by applying the skills. Throughout, students are encouraged to identify where they are in their learning and what their next steps will be. Using familiar assessment for learning strategies, the teacher can also gather and review secure evidence of day-to-day progress in each strand.

The examples and activities within the reading series aim to support students to develop key decoding and comprehension skills, including using a range of strategies to read for meaning, finding information, inferring and deducing and understanding writers' use of language and structure. Within the writing series, students are encouraged not only to expand the grammatical constructions they use but also to add descriptive power to their vocabulary, resulting in more imaginative, interesting and thoughtful writing.

Building on the success of the original *Aiming for...* series, this latest edition covers the 2014 curriculum. Chapters have been updated to include coverage of the Key Stage 3 Programme of Study and the Grammar, Vocabulary and Punctuation Appendix to the Key Stage 2 Programme of Study.

At the end of each chapter, the two sets of progress statements enable students to assess themselves, deciding if they have made good or excellent progress in the session. These statements have been designed to parallel the existing national curriculum levels, where good progress demonstrates the student is working at a low/secure level 3 *within the skills addressed in the session*, and excellent progress demonstrates a secure/high level 3.

The Teacher Guide section of this latest edition has also been updated and provides essential advice on how teachers can support students to make great progress in English. Although the *Aiming for...* books are designed for students to use with a level of independence, it is particularly important that, as students are developing their skills at this earlier level, the teacher is able to assess and mediate this process as appropriate. The Teacher Guide includes additional starter activities that provide an opportunity to secure the underlying knowledge students will need in order to tackle the focused activities successfully.

Natalie Packer

Series Editor

Starter

Change a letter

Allow your students to work in pairs. You might want them to work together or they could play the activity as a game and compete to see who can come up with more words. Start by giving them the following words:

hen

wag

tab

rag

tag

The full range of phenomes can be found listed here:

http://www.lancsngfl.ac.uk/curriculum/literacy/lit_site/lit_sites/phonemes_001/

Now ask your students to change the first letter of each word from the list to make a new word. For example

hen can become den

wag can become bag

tab can become cab

rag can become hag

tag can become lag

Now ask them to think of a letter they could place in front of each word to make new words. For example

t-hen = then

s-wag = swag

s-tab = stab

b-rag = brag

s-tag = stag

1 Use a range of strategies to read tricky words

Getting you thinking

Model the poem by reading it to students. Encourage students to look at the pictures and, working in pairs or groups, tease out what the poem is about. They should work out that although the son realises his dad is a 'good bloke', he doesn't want his dad embarrassing him in front of his friends.

How does it work?

Students could list the words they don't know and then look them up in a dictionary. For example, if they do not know the word 'ridiculous', they should look up the first letter (r), then the second letter (i), then the third (d), and so on. They should sound out the word as they go. As they sound out the word, students who are comfortable with the alphabet should be able to find it and its definition in a dictionary.

Students can also try to sound out the word like this:

- They can start with the initial letter but if they still do not know the word, ask them to sound out the middle or end letters.

- After sounding out the word, ask them to blend the sounds together to try and say the word.

- Finally, ask your students if the word makes sense in the context of the line in the poem.

For longer, harder words, such as 'impressions', help your students to break the word into manageable chunks. Remind students of the following strategies to help them with tricky words:

- using sentence context
- using picture cues
- breaking words into syllables
- looking for familiar patterns and endings.

Now you try it
Allow students to read the poem on their own. They should work out that

2 Dad performed a ridiculous dance.

3 The son would pay his dad to hide when he (the son) had friends round.

Ensure that students give reasons for their answers to Activity 4.

Apply your skills
Ask your students to jot down at least eight bullet points. They are, in effect, learning to summarise the poem.

2 Read independently and with understanding

Getting you thinking
Students should be able to use a range of strategies (see page 80, *How does it work?*) to read the words they find difficult.

Now you try it
Students should work out that

a) The jackets were black.

b) The gang was called the Hood Gang.

c) The writer thinks the gang will get caught.

Apply your skills
Your students should work out that the sentences they need to copy are b, c and e.

3 Read with confidence and expression

How does it work?
Your students will need to know how to vary their tone, volume and facial expressions based on clues in the text. These techniques will enable them to reflect the emotions expressed in the text and to emphasise particular words.

Model varying your tone of voice. Tell your students to read slower than they would normally speak – to show emotions such as exasperation, excitement, boredom and relief in their voices. They can change the volume of their voices from quiet to loud – and a whisper can be very effective!

Facial expressions are important. For example, a smile, frown or a look of disgust can have a big impact.

The way we stand can also have an effect – a certain posture can show the listeners how they are meant to understand the text.

Apply your skills
There are a number of ways for students to record their readings. Here are some tips to give your students:

- Make sure you are ready and confident.

- Remember to vary your tone.

- If you are recording only your voice – that is all the audience have. You therefore need to speak clearly and use lots of expression.

- If you are videoing your reading, remember to use facial expressions and, if appropriate, posture and hand gestures.

Starter 1

Ways of moving

This activity needs a large space such as a school hall or drama room. As a quick warm-up, ask students to try these different ways of moving:

- walking
- walking with a limp
- crawling
- rolling
- hopping
- skipping
- jumping
- leaping
- walking on tiptoe
- walking backwards.

Then encourage them to think about different ways of walking:

- Allow students to **walk** around the space as they wish. Some may march, others stride, and others may walk slowly or quickly.

- Then ask them to walk as **slowly** as they can. Then ask them to walk, with care, as quickly as they can. They can then walk with a limp.

- Then ask them to walk as **high** as they can – on tiptoe.

- They can then walk as **low** as they can – by slouching.

- They can walk as **lightly** as they can (like a ballet dancer) or as heavily as they can (like a footballer who's just scored an own goal or been sent off).

- Students can then walk **directly** – from point to point. Or they can walk

indirectly – wandering aimlessly, say with hands in pockets.

- They can change the **focus** of the movement, meaning they can alter their facial expressions and gaze. Usually, this automatically changes their body curve.

- They can then think of an unhappy person – walking aimlessly, perhaps staring at the floor; or a person in a hurry, eyes fixed forward; or a happy person, who might stride out, chin up.

In this Starter activity, choose students who do particularly well and allow them to model their work to the rest of the group.

Explain to students that they have 'been' different characters. Our facial expressions, body language and the way we move show others our personality and our mood. Allow one student to model being happy. As the group watch, ask them the following questions:

- How do we know the character is happy? Is the character (or student name) walking quickly or slowly? Is the student looking ahead or glaring at the floor? Is the student walking heavily or lightly?

Students should then recognise what a happy or sad person would be like.

Ask individual students to model other emotions – such as anger, being upset, frightened or excited.

Tell them they are going to look at and write about different characters. When they write about characters, they need to think about how the characters would walk, talk, think and behave – depending on their moods.

Erik the Red

Greenland is a cold place of ice and snow, so do you know how it got the name 'Greenland'? It is because a Viking named Erik the Red had an argument with the king of Iceland. He was banished from Iceland and had to discover a new land.

Erik set sail and discovered this cold land of ice and frosts. He wanted other people to live with him in this new land, so he called it Greenland. Greenland sounds more inviting than Iceland, so others joined Erik. They soon discovered that this new land was far from green!

Read this passage to your students, then give them a copy. Model the skill of summarising by giving them one or two of the bullet points below. Then, as a group, finish the summary verbally.

- Greenland is a place of ice and snow.

- Erik the Red was banished by the king of Iceland.

- Erik discovered a new land.

- He called the new land Greenland.

- Others joined him but were disappointed.

1 Find and summarise information from a non-fiction text

Getting you thinking

Remind students of the differences between fiction and non-fiction. You might want to bring examples in to show them.

Model the extract by reading it to the students. Show students a map of Australia. Point out Melbourne in the south and show them how far Robert Burke and the team had to trek to reach the north coast.

Students should use key words in the questions to support their scanning. The answers to the questions are as follows.

a) Ireland

b) The army

c) The police

d) Sometimes it was boring

e) It might bring fame and fortune

f) He'd never explored before and he'd never led a team.

Try to persuade your students to write using full sentences.

Now you try it

2   An example sentence for the first paragraph might be: Robert Burke decided to explore unknown Australia, walking from the south to the north.

3   Your students should now have four sentences. You could challenge them to summarise the four sentences in one – still giving the vital information!

Apply your skills

4   If students cannot work out Robert Burke's mistakes, point them out:

- He didn't stop for water.

- He made the team march for 16 hours a day.

5   Explain to students what 'hot seating' is and ensure that they use the evidence in the text to build up a picture of Robert Burke's character.

2 Select information to make decisions about characters

Getting you thinking

1 The answers are: **a)** Shelley Collit **b)** Emma Harman **c)** Shelley Collit

2 Students should be able to show their partners how they found their answers: **a)** dogs, guinea pig and rabbit **b)** hip hop (plus the picture shows her wearing headphones) **c)** Jason is described as 'tall and thin', Jeremy as 'average height, a bit overweight' and Emma 'blonde'.

Now you try it

The answers depend upon the student's ideas of friendship. However, they will need to back up their ideas using evidence from the text.

For an extension activity, ask students to be one of the four characters and 'hot seat' that character. Staying in role, students have to defend their characters, thinking about their way of life and how they behave.

Students could then write an imagined event in the life of their character.

Example: Jason Smart

- Jason takes a ten-pound note from the maths teacher's pocket.

- The maths teacher realises his money has gone. He is upset, as he needed the ten-pound note to buy his daughter a birthday present.

- The class is sympathetic but they don't know who has taken the money.

- It's break time and the class files out of the classroom.

- Jim Fullerton, a member of Jason's class, knows Jason is a pickpocket. He confronts Jason, who denies taking any money. He claims he has no money with him.

- At the dining hall, Jason is spotted buying lots of food and drink. He is about to hand the money over to the dinner lady. Jim and the rest of his class surround him. Students tell him he is mean and wrong and they'll tell the maths teacher he has stolen the money.

- Jason pleads with his peers and they agree to a plan.

- Jason finds the maths teacher, and tells him he went back to the maths room and searched for the money. He discovered the ten-pound note stuffed behind a radiator.

- The maths teacher is thankful and praises Jason!

When students write or bullet point their story, they must they must remain in role as their character. They should be able to justify why they think the character would act in this way.

Apply your skills

There are usually pointers in films or books to give you clues about characters. For example, a bad character might snap and scowl, or say things that show what kind of person they are. We can find out about characters by paying attention to what they do, what they say and how they say it, how they treat other characters and how other characters treat them, and how they are directly described by the author.

3 Describe and understand characters in fiction

Getting you thinking
Model the story by reading it to students. Possible answers your students might give for the questions are

a) She thinks he gets into bother.

b) He kicked the football through the school window and threw the chewing gum into Chelsea's hair.

c) He has to behave. This is his last chance.

d) He thinks he's just unlucky.

e) No (see the answer to b).

Now you try it
Possible answers to the questions are

a) They seem to be snobs (they look down their noses at MacDuff). They are (he says) teacher's pets. He also implies they might be bullies (to Gary).

b) He does what Tom and Alex tell him to do.

c) They see MacDuff as trouble, or perhaps they realise they can't bully him as they bully Gary.

Apply your skills
Encourage your students to look for evidence in the text to carry out the activities.

3   Your students should work out that

- Gary Bond appears to be a 'yes' boy. He'll do whatever the other boys ask him to do ('How high?'). He wants to stay 'in' with them.

- Mr Hoss appears stern/strict. ('Behave, or else'). He firmly tells MacDuff that the trip is his 'last chance'.

- Macduff is always in trouble – even his mother asks him to make her proud 'for once'. The 'for once' suggests she's rarely proud of him. It implies he's in trouble a lot. The 'somebody' who kicked the ball through the window is obviously him. He tries to make excuses for his wrongdoing. He tries to claim the chewing gum in the hair incident was not his fault.

4   Your students should work out that the writer has made the characters different but also that all the characters are seen through MacDuff's eyes (from his point of view). He tells us what they (and he) say and do. He implies that he's unlucky but the reader can see that this is not quite true!

Chapter 3   Deduce, infer or interpret information, events or ideas from texts

Starter

What would you do?
Students take on the role of a character. The character can be invented or can be a famous person known to all. You ask the student: 'What would the character do if…?'

- The character saw a derelict building and walked into it, and noticed somebody slumped on a chair. (Students can mime walking into the building and mime what they would do.)

- The person slumped on the chair has their face cast downwards, so you can't see who it is. What would you do? (Again, the student can mime the action.)

- Whatever you thought you would do, you actually go up to the person and lift up their face. Then you get a shock – you are looking at yourself! (The student can mime the action.)

It is a good idea to get all the students working on this at the same time. The aim of the exercise is to allow students to work out how a character might feel in a particular situation. It should put them in others' shoes before they write anything.

1 Work out the meaning of a poem

Getting you thinking
Read the poem to your students. Ask your students to decide if the first four verses are about the poet's past, present or future. How can they tell? Ask them to pick out anything they like about the poem. Why do they like a particular line? What does it mean to them?

Now you try it
Possible answers are

2   The boy, who is now grown up. The poet.

3   The man is from the future. He is the poet.

4   The boy, or the boy in the poet's imagination.

Apply your skills
Allow students to work in pairs. Possible answers are

5   They all grew up. The word 'Time' gives us the clue.

6   'Evermore' is basically our memories of the past.

7   'Nostalgic'. (Allow 'Very sad'.) You might want to explain that nostalgic describes a longing or affectionate feeling for the past.

2 Understand feelings through performance poetry

Getting you thinking
Model the poem for the students by reading it to them, using two voices. The students should work out that the conversation is between a student (Blenkinsop) and his teacher.

How does it work?
This poem should give your students confidence in their reading, as they do not have to read many lines at a time. Explain to the students how you can make the teacher's voice different from Blenkinsop's voice when you read the poem. Discuss how the poet makes the poem funny by listing all Blenkinsop's ridiculous excuses.

Now you try it
Students should work out that

2   a) The teacher seems amused at Blenkinsop's excuses.

   b) Blenkinsop is hoping he'll get out of PE.

3   a) Blenkinsop appears to win the argument because he gets out of the PE lesson.

   b) He must dislike PE because he's making excuses to get out of it.

   c) Students might think the poem is funny or clever. They should be able to give reasons for the words they choose to describe it.

4 The teacher's tone of voice might be good-humoured at first – but change after line 24 to become more and more exasperated.

Apply your skills

Students need to decide who will be the teacher and who will be Blenkinsop. They should think about how the teacher would react at first and how he would react towards the end of the poem – when Blenkinsop is trying to get out of his PE lesson. Would Blenkinsop use a voice that is mildly teasing the teacher – so the teacher is unaware of Blenkinsop's teasing? Or would he appear triumphant when he says his last few lines? Or would he hide his emotions from the teacher? Students should be allowed a few tries at the poem until they are happy with their performance.

As an extra task, your students could draw both characters and add thought bubbles for both as the poem progresses.

3 Draw conclusions about events, character and ideas from a play extract

Getting you thinking

The students will need to be in groups of four. You may wish to model the play before your students try it themselves, adopting different voices for the four characters.

Possible answers to the questions are as follows.

a) A block of flats.

b) Ethan hopes to hide from the gang. Even in this situation, he uses humour ('heat-seeking device') – or is he half-serious?

c) He is afraid – he stutters. He pleads for them to let him go.

d) Aiden suggests tasks for Ethan and tells Lucas, in no uncertain terms, that he's the boss.

e) If your students cannot think of any ideas, feed this one to them: perhaps Lucas will challenge Aiden – Ethan might then escape. Any workable suggestion, based on evidence from the play, would be fine.

You could also ask your students how the playwright keeps the suspense going. They should work out that

- Ethan is afraid before he is caught.
- He stutters when caught, so we wonder what will happen to him.
- We do not know what the secret is, but it must be dangerous, as Lucas challenged Aiden's decision. We have a clue – it is something to do with a car.

All these factors keep the suspense going. As readers, we can empathise with Ethan. We can almost imagine we are in his situation, which makes the play exciting.

Now you try it

Your students need to back up their ideas using evidence from the text.

Apply your skills

Your students need to think of the play's themes – for example, gangs, bullying, authority (and challenges to bad authority) and fear. Or they can suggest other themes, as long as they can back up their suggestions with evidence from the play.

Starter

Making a story more exciting

Give your students this story with the gaps in it and the word bank (or put them on the board). In groups, students can play the game to fill in the gaps and make the story more exciting. The first time, they can go round in a group, using the words from the word bank. The second time, they could use their own words to fill the gaps. If anyone goes wrong or can't think of a word, they are out of the game.

One _____ night, I was visiting my _____ gran. She lived in a _____ house. I knocked _____ on the door.

I could hear a _____ noise along the corridor. The door opened _____. There was a _____ stranger standing looking down at me.

dark	frail	tumbledown	spooky
gloomy	old	loudly	rustling	slowly
	sharply	sinister	horrid

1 Understand what makes an exciting start to a story

Getting you thinking

1   Ensure that students give reasons for their decisions.

2   The students will need to give reasons for their answers. You might want to give them prompts such as

  • Do they all set the scene?

  • Do they all introduce characters?

  • Do they all make you want to read on?

Now you try it

You might want to explain what is happening in the story:

  • The story is told to us by a monkey – later on in the story we find out his name is Giz.

  • Giz is talking about a new arrival named Skink.

  • Giz mentions how to 'whoop' and he tells us how it is done.

  • Giz has a favourite tree; it's called the Big Tree. We discover that Giz does not like spending time with the other monkeys. He likes being alone, thinking.

  • We then discover that Giz is not free: he is in an enclosure. He is fenced in. This comes as a bit of a shock.

  • Giz has a friend, called Chim. Chim believes Giz is spending too much time thinking. Chim believes that thinking is dangerous. He warns Giz that if he spends too much time thinking, he'll end up wearing his brains out!

Ask the students what they think might happen next. Students could get into groups and work out what sort of a character Skink might be. Why will he be mighty?

3   Most students will work out the following:

  a)   A monkey.

b) Skink arrived. The reader will want to know who Skink is and why he has 'changed things forever'.

c) Students might find 'whoop' funny. Also, the idea that thinking can wear a brain out is amusing.

4 a) The setting is quickly established by use of the words 'Enclosure' and 'The Fence'. We learn that the monkeys are not free.

b) The fact that these words start with a capital letter suggests that captivity is an important part of their lives and it will be an issue in the book.

c) 'Chattering' describes the sound the monkeys make; 'scoot' describes the way they move.

As an additional exercise, you might like to give your students the following sentence:

Skink runs around the big, leafy tree.

Point out that 'Skink' and 'tree' are naming words, so they are nouns. 'Runs' is a doing word, so it is a verb. 'Big' and 'leafy' tell us something about the tree. They are adjectives.

5 Possible answers might be that you want to find out who Skink is, why Skink's arrival meant things changed forever, and whether the monkeys will always be captive. The interesting use of language and the humour might make students want to read on, too.

Apply your skills
Your students could jot down their ideas in the form of a spider diagram to 'thought shower' ideas before they draft out their speech.

2 Understand what makes an amazing middle

Getting you thinking
Explain to students the story so far: Amelia has bunked off school. She arrives home and is in her bedroom when her dad arrives. She sneaks a look downstairs. In the hallway are her dad and two strangers. They argue and threaten her dad. Her dad sounds frightened. Later, her dad vanishes. Amelia goes in search of him. She finally stops in a café to think what to do next. Then model the story by reading it to the students.

Your students might provide the following possible answers:

1 She doesn't know what's happened to her dad.

2 Mysteriously, the waiter knows who Amelia is and he also knows about her dad.

Now you try it
Students should work out that 'hissed' sounds sinister or threatening. Amelia does not trust the waiter, even though he smiles at her. His smile doesn't 'seem real'. The fact that she shivers shows that he makes her feel physically uncomfortable or frightened.

Apply your skills
The second extract includes more description and gives us more information. Shorter paragraphs are easier to follow and make the action more exciting and immediate.

3 Understand what makes an awesome end

Getting you thinking
Ask your students if they think introducing characters later on in the story is a good idea.

Now you try it
3   Another ending could be

- Amelia walks out of the café and spots a policeman.

- The waiter is questioned and informs on the gang.

- The gang members are arrested.

- Amelia's dad is found hiding at a friend's house.

Can your students think of other alternative endings? Perhaps they can work in pairs to think of a more exciting ending? Students could then act out their alternative scenarios.

Some students might not be able to sustain a story ending and may need reminders. They could work in pairs and storyboard or spider-diagram their ideas.

Apply your skills
Encourage students to read their ideas for a story end to each other. They should choose the best ideas and act the story end out if possible.

Chapter 5   Explain and comment on writers' use of language, including grammatical and literary features at word and sentence level

These starters are based on the belief that children know a great deal about the structure and conventions of stories. The activities are based on the premise that literature is something to be thought about and talked about, not just consumed. They aim to develop students' understanding of texts and the societies which produced them and in which they are read.

This chapter focuses on the language used in traditional and modern versions of fairy tales. Traditional tales often use words such as 'bewitched', 'wicked' and 'enchanted'. Point out that these words are not exclusive to fairy tales but are often found within fairy tales. Can your students think of other examples?

Starter 1

Once upon a time…
Start by asking students how traditional stories usually begin. They should know that most begin with 'Once upon a time…'.

Allow students to sit in a circle. Start the game by saying 'Once upon a time…there lived a wicked witch.'

Tell students they have to say what happened next.

> **Example**:
> You: Once upon a time there lived a wicked witch.

> Student 1: She liked to eat people.

> Student 2: First she captured a young boy.

> Student 3: Next she put him in a cooking pot.

> Student 4: But he managed to escape.

You might want to complete the story.

> You: The witch fell into her own pot and was boiled!

Starter 2

Not long ago…
You could then try a modern story.

> You: Not long ago – a gang roamed the streets.

These two starter exercises should give students a sense of story structure.

Starter 3

Tell a fairy tale
Ask your students what fairy tales they know. Remind them of 'Little Red Riding Hood', 'Goldilocks and the Three Bears' or 'Jack and the Beanstalk'.

Tell them that these stories have been around for centuries. They were told even before they were written down. Many of the stories are known throughout the world in different versions.

In groups, ask them to tell each other a fairy tale. Remind them about eye contact, tone of voice, pace, volume and body language. You may want them to have the following information:

- **Eye contact** – Look at other people in your group now and again. It helps to keep their attention.

- **Tone of voice** – Vary your tone of voice. This will stop people in the group becoming bored.

- **Pace** – Avoid speaking too slowly or too quickly.

- **Volume** – Speak loudly enough to be heard, without shouting. Try to speak using expression in your voice.

- **Body language** – Look confident. Use a few hand gestures.

1 Understand and comment on the writer's use of language in a traditional tale

Getting you thinking
Read 'The Princess and the Frog' to your students. Students may spot the fairy-tale conventions. If not, point them out in the story. Possible answers to the questions are

1 'Once upon a time', 'big castle', 'handsome prince', 'lived happily ever after'.

2 **a)** king, frog, crown

  b) played, croaked, bewitched

  c) big, golden, ugly

  d) suddenly, carefully, happily

How does it work?
You might like to read the start of one or two traditional fairy tales to your students.

Now you try it
Most school libraries will have a book of traditional fairy tales; if not, there are plenty of examples on the Internet.

Apply your skills

5 Show students the underlined words and explain why the author has chosen to use them. Students can use a thesaurus to find words similar in meaning, but remind them that a thesaurus is not a dictionary. They may need to check the meaning of the word they have chosen in their dictionaries.

2 Understand and comment on the writer's use of language in a modern tale

Getting you thinking
Model the story to the students by reading it to them. Explain to students that as you read the story you want them to notice how the language differs from the first extract. Ask them what makes it a modern story.

1 The start and ending still tell you when the story is set and what happened at the end, but the words used are very different. The story is modern so it is set 'Not long ago' and instead of living happily ever after, the prince is nagged to death!

Now you try it
You may wish to give students copies of the two versions. Allow them to pick out the modern words. They could make a chart.

2 Possible words and phrases are 'spoilt brat', 'outdoor swimming pool', 'Yeah, whatever!', 'He'd do!'

3 Students should be able to give reasons for their choices.

Apply your skills
Students can choose a tale they have already found in the library or on the Internet. Once they have planned how to turn the traditional tale into a modern one, they can read it to a partner. Remind students that, when they are giving feedback, their suggested changes should always be positive and improve the story.

Chapter 6   Identify and comment on writers' purposes and viewpoints, and the overall effect of the text on the reader

Starter 1

Fact or viewpoint?
Allow students to sit in a circle. Ask them to say something that is true. For example

- Our uniform is blue.
- The sun warms planet Earth.
- I have a pet dog.
- Our desks are made of wood.

Now ask students to say something that is a point of view. For example:

- Andy Murray is the best tennis player in the world.
- My mum's the best mum ever.

- Science lessons are a waste of time.
- Motorbikes are better than cars.
- The world will end in 20 years' time.

Point out that viewpoints are a matter of opinion. They might be true but they often aren't!

Ask students to decide, in small groups, which of the following statements are true and which are not:

- Being at school is a waste of time.
- All dogs chase cats.
- On Saturday we don't go to school.

- Cod is a type of fish.
- Cabbage tastes awful.

Allow students to send one member to another group. Have both groups got the same answers? Ask students to discuss their answers and see if they can reach agreement.

Starter 2

Agree or disagree?
In pairs, students should express viewpoints about their likes and dislikes.

A says a viewpoint and **B** agrees or disagrees. After five minutes, they swap roles.

Example:

A: I don't like getting up in the mornings.

B: Neither do I. It's a right pain, isn't it?

A: But I enjoy school. Lessons are fun.

B: I can't agree. I don't enjoy school – except games.

A: I like reading non-fiction. I like finding out about things.

And so on…

1 Identify different viewpoints

Getting you thinking
1   Your students should identify Joanne, Aisha and Wayne as the three who give reasons for their views – although Wayne has not mentioned why Maths is fun.

Now you try it
2   Possible answers are

'Children shouldn't have too much time on the computer because it's important to do active things as well.'

'Many dogs are gentle and well trained and so don't need to be kept on a lead.'

'The football manager picks the team so it is the manager's fault if the team is doing badly.'

'Separating bullies won't stop them bullying. They need to learn what they're doing is wrong and say sorry.'

Apply your skills
The following texts are the most likely to include a writer's viewpoint:
- A letter to a friend
- A newspaper article about a film.

2 Comment on writers' purposes and viewpoints, and the effect of the text on the reader

Getting you thinking
Possible answers to the questions are as follows.

1   Your students are a disgrace. Their uniforms are a mess. You should check them and send your students home if they are scruffy.

2   He has used strong adjectives such as 'horrible' and 'scruffy'. He has also used a strong verb – 'demand', rather than 'ask'. He uses exaggeration to get his point across: 'All teenagers are horrible' and 'your students are worse'. Perhaps some students are scruffy but it is unlikely they all are. Finally, the words 'In my view' show that this is his viewpoint.

Apply your skills
a)   Students can pick either of the two letters but they must give reasons for their choice.

b) Again, students need to be able to pick out words and phrases that they found persuasive. Perhaps the forceful words in the Desmond Worldwise letter or the more emotive words in the Sonya Harper letter, such as 'After all, you want your kids to stay fit and healthy, don't you?'

Chapter 7   Relate texts to their social, cultural and historical traditions

Starter

Features of storytelling
In this chapter, students will be asked to tell a local story. Ask them for their ideas about how to tell a story. Then give them the tips below:

- Remember, storytelling is an art. It is also 'interactive'. This means you are telling and others are listening and responding.

- Face the group of people you are telling the story to.

- Before you start telling your story – wait for silence. Wait until everyone is looking at you. Tell your story as if it is actually happening to you or to someone you know well.

- Try to create an atmosphere. For example, if you are telling a ghost story, you could possibly turn down (or turn off) the lights.

- When you begin, let your eyes move slowly around your audience. Keep eye contact all the time you're telling the story. Use your hands and face to show feelings. Use your voice – make sure you can be heard. Change your pace and volume. Don't forget to pause for dramatic effect. Try to begin in a dramatic way. This means you need an exciting start.

- Keep your listeners interested. Keep them wondering what will happen next. Build up to a dramatic ending. **Example**: (*Silence*) … Ohhhh… (*Bang your fists on the table*) …Ahhhhh… (*Dramatic pause*) The arrow buried deep into his chest. (*Dramatic pause*) The king was dead! (*Pause*) The enemy had won. (*Bang on desk three times*) The enemy horses galloped through the ranks of soldiers. (*Dramatic pause*) 'Run, run,' yelled the captain.

1 Recognise stories from the past, present, future and other places

Getting you thinking
The students should work out the following:

The Passenger is set in the present; *Gladiator* is set in the past (they might also guess it is in another country); *The Name is Kade* is set in the future and possibly on another planet; *Bound for Jamaica* is set in the past and in another country.

Now you try it
Students should be encouraged to look for clues to help them answer the questions.

2 **a)** The past.

  b) The title *In Ancient Time*, the story round the fire and the mention of being a young man before the Romans came.

3 a) St Petersburg, Russia, probably in the present or not-very-distant past.

b) We are told the story is set in St Petersburg. The car horns in rush-hour traffic tell us it is probably set in the present day.

4 a) On another planet, in the future.

b) 'We had landed', 'blue creature' and 'weird, spiky plants' tell us the story is set in the future on a different planet.

Apply your skills
Tell students they should put in clues so that their partner can guess if the story is set in the past/present/future or in a different place.

2 Recognise a local story

Getting you thinking
Possible answers are

1 a) The land is flat. It is known as Fenland. The setting is the countryside, not far from the sea.

b) 'Sluss' and 'highlows'. Explain that dialect words are specific to a region or local area. You could also ask if students can think of any dialect words from their own area.

c) Suspense. Words such as 'nervous', 'dark', 'gloomy', and phrases such as 'shivers down my spine'. There is a moan, a rustling sound and a door handle turns – but there is nobody in the corridor.

2 You might wish to tease out some features of a ghost story. For example: often set at night/isolated house or room/a shadow/noises/light knocks/rustling sounds/bad weather.

Now you try it
Ask students 'Do you know a local story?' Encourage them to tell it. Then ask them to bullet point the main parts of the story, in a logical order. They should jot down the most important information. Then they can practise speaking it aloud to themselves. After a try, they might want to improve their story. Ask your students, 'Is there anything you've missed?' Now they can retell the story to a partner. Before they do, remind them of the features of storytelling (see Starter on page 94).

Notes